Letting Go of

Focus on Faith

Envy

Patti Normile

Path of Life Publications
Spiritual Food for the Christian Journey from Abbey Press

Introduction

The color green has long been associated with envy for good reason. Sick persons sometimes look pale, perhaps tinged with a sickly hue of green. Emotional, physical, and spiritual illness can arise from unbridled envy, thus the envy-green connection.

Because envy can be a serious malady, it is often referred to as a *deadly* sin. The frightening deadliness of extreme envy is revealed on those tragic occasions when a love relationship ends, and the jilted person kills the one who has been lost. Likewise, school shootings often occur as the result of the shooter envying the popularity of others to a deadly degree.

These are extreme examples, of course, but ordinary family hostilities can fume when siblings feel unfairness exists in family relationships. Friends may become estranged when one acquires a new friend, and the old friend feels left out. Workplace antagonism can be fostered when a co-worker receives a promotion for which another had hoped.

So, what are the symptoms of envy? Envy is marked by an unquenchable desire for what another person possesses or is perceived to have. That desire may focus on material possessions and wealth, physical traits such as beauty or athleticism, musical or artistic talents, relationship skills, plus a myriad of other qualities or possessions that one person has and another desires. Thomas Aquinas described envy as "sorrow for another's good."

Resentment and anger arise when envy is not recognized and addressed. The envier may become obsessed with what she perceives as her lack of what another has. Envy can hold the individual in its grip like a vice—grasping and unrelenting.

Seeking the source and healing the wound of envy is essential to happiness. This book aims to help you do both. After all, God desires the happiness of us all (cf. Psalm 37:4; 84:12).

Lacking belief in one's own worth plants seeds of envy. When one feels inadequate, falling into the trap of envy is a grave danger.

Being realistic conquers the temptation to envy. Michael says, "I've never envied what I couldn't have. I was born wanting things I couldn't have. I just work harder than the normal person to get what I want. I have never been jealous of something I knew I couldn't have." Michael believes in himself and works to achieve what he desires.

*You are
at **peace**
in the
hermitage
of **yourself**.*

— *Larry McMurtry*, By Sorrow's River

Who am I, Lord? Please show me who I am deep inside the hermitage of myself. When I realize that I am your creation—fearfully, wonderfully made—I am free to be myself. I am free to grow into the person you have created me to be. I need not covet what others possess. I only need to grow into my own true being. Amen.

Because envy is not at all an admirable trait, we tend to avoid even considering that it might lurk within ourselves. "Me? Envious? No way!" Reality indicates, however, that envy may sneak past our personal defenses when we least expect it.

How can we recognize the initial promptings of envy? An appreciative look or thought directed toward what another possesses can raise a thought: "Why should *he* have such good luck, and I don't?" Be honest. Envy has often reared its unpleasant head. Admitting it is the only way to successfully resist it.

the Spirit helps us
in our weakness;
for we do not know
how to pray as we ought,
but that very Spirit
intercedes with sighs
too deep for words.

—Romans 8:26

Focus on Faith

Lord, I don't want to become scrupulous, but I do ask your guidance in recognizing times when appreciation for what another person possesses might evolve into envy. Please keep me mindful, Lord. Amen.

Susan's friendship with Jane had changed. Whenever they gathered with friends, Jane snipped and snapped at Susan, attempting to make her look inferior. It was puzzling until a friend observed, "She's envious of you, Susan. You're attractive, happily married, great kids, well-educated—while she is struggling."

Perhaps you can recognize such circumstances in some of your own relationships. Like Susan, you can choose not to react to such possible manifestations of envy, and act instead with self-assured kindness.

In everything,
do to others
as you
would have
them do to you.

—Matthew 7:12

Do I act or react when another person either subtly or harshly attempts to harm my sense of self-worth? Help me, Lord, to use that old method of counting to 10 while waiting to act rather than quickly reacting. What is the source of the other's animosity? It might be envy. What part can I play in remedying that?

Envy and jealousy are similar, yet there is a distinction between them. Jealousy stems from fear that what we *have* might be taken from us—whether it is a relationship, a position, or a possession. Therefore, jealousy can dampen relationships. Generosity, or the willingness to share what we may hold dear, removes the grasping tendency of jealousy.

Envy, on the other hand, involves what we perceive to *not have*. Seeing a quality or a possession that belongs to another that we may feel we lack can arouse envy. Gratitude is the antidote for envy—reflect on the gifts and talents we are blessed to possess, and thank God for them.

Job found **peace**
only when he
stopped obsessing
and comparing
his life with others.
He **let go and**
let God be God.

—*Michael Leach*,
"Soul Seeing," National Catholic Reporter

Am I willing to remember that God is God and I am not? In what ways might I relinquish my "godly" ways of entertaining envy for the job my neighbor got, the house my brother bought, the friendships others seem to cultivate? I need your help, Lord, to recognize and to relinquish feelings of envy and jealousy. You alone provide what I need. Amen.

From toddler years to adulthood, people commented on Patty's beauty. Those comments stung her sister, Madeleine. She was unable to treasure her own unique beauty because of the envy she felt for Patty's extraordinary good looks.

Despite these feelings, when Patty developed multiple sclerosis, Madeleine ministered to her sister—giving massages, and caring in every way. Caring conquered envy, and the inner beauty of both sisters truly emerged.

If there were no envy,
but only love—
if each should count
and feel his neighbor's
good to be his own gain,
this earth would
already be a heaven.

— *William Arnot,*
Illustrations of the Book of Proverbs

What we see can sometimes deceive us into undervaluing ourselves, thereby producing envy. When we see another's physical beauty, we must not judge our own to be less. Look for the beauty within—within others and within ourselves. Look into a mirror. Who do you see? Hopefully, you will see a wondrous person created in God's own image.

Jason noticed that his fists were clenched when his friend Sam had decisively beaten him in a round of golf—again!

Such moments offer us a critical opportunity to choose what is good, and to let go of the temptation to give in to envy. Positive self-talk is especially helpful: "It's only a game. He's your friend! You didn't play badly. He just played better." When envy is recognized and addressed, and is accompanied with a genuine appreciation for the other, we are the clear winners.

Strive first
for the kingdom
of God
and all these things
will be given
to you as well.

—Matthew 6:33

Whatever goodness or beauty is added to the world—a lovely painting, athletic ability, a voice that sings like an angel, plumbing skills, compassion for others—makes the world a better place. I will treasure the goodness, grace, and gifts of others.

Trudging up a mountain, Moses dared to approach God; lugging heavy stone tablets inscribed with a way of life, he went back down the mountain. What awaited him? God's people, so gripped by envy of the gods that others worshipped that they made a golden calf to worship. The tablets shattered on the ground as Moses expressed fury at the worshipping of an idol.

Similarly, an angry Jesus overturned tables in the Temple in Jerusalem. The money-changers, envying the way that other entrepreneurs exploited worshippers, had created a "den of thieves." God wishes us to be free of the idols that envy can produce.

You shall not
covet [envy]
your neighbor's house;
You shall not
covet [envy]
your neighbor's wife,
or anything
that belongs
to your neighbor.

—*Exodus 20:17*

We may scoff at the idea of a golden calf, but do we indeed have our own modern idols of worship? Do we spend more time praying to God or viewing sports events? Do we spend as much time listening to God as we spend watching televised news? Good and Loving God, show me where my golden calves are tethered. Amen.

Love is patient, love is kind Love does not seek its own Love believes all things Bears all things

Not all envy is sinister. Envy may initially emerge as genuine appreciation for the ability, appearance, or possession of another person. Yes, we might like to be as patient as someone appears to be, or to be as wise as another seems. Striving after such virtue when inspired by another is a good thing.

Such genuine, motivational appreciation becomes tinged with the evil of envy only if we become preoccupied with another's quality, or tend to discredit the genuine gift of the other.

If we live by the Spirit,
let us also be
guided by the Spirit.
Let us not
become conceited,
competing against
one another,
envying one another.

—Galatians 5:25-26

If discerning between genuine appreciation and the evil of envy challenges you, your feelings may offer a clue. Are you genuinely happy for the gift or ability of the other individual? If you desire a certain quality or possession for yourself, why is that? If the answer is to make oneself superior and the other inferior, envy may be the culprit.

Perhaps you've detected a hint of envy in your attitude. Congratulatory words stuck in your throat when your friend told you about his new job. Recognizing envy is crucial to nipping it in the bud. So, name it—*envy!*

Now it's treatment time. Examine the source of your envy. Would the thing you wish for enhance your life—or do you simply regret that *another person* possesses it? Cultivating a thankful spirit is healing. Thank God for the other's gift that prompted your feeling of envy. Then let it go—with thanksgiving.

What does the lord
require of you
but to do justice,
and to love kindness,
and to walk humbly
with your god?

—*Micah 6:8*

Focus on Faith

A thankful spirit is a humble spirit.
A humble spirit allows God's presence
to grow within me. If what prompted
my envy would improve life for myself
and others, I will work to achieve it.
God will provide what I need. I will
provide my cooperation and my
willingness to thank God for
everyone's gifts.

If you have appendicitis or an abscessed tooth, removal is essential for good health. If afflicted by envy, diagnosis and removal are necessary for spiritual, emotional, and even physical health. Untreated, envy will fester. Envy sickens relationships. It affects self-esteem, even work performance. Acute envy may even make us ill.

The longer envy is left untreated, the deeper it can infect our lives. Denial is not healing. Honesty with oneself and with God will root out envy's devastating effects.

*Envy is called
a passion;
and means suffering.
Envy is a
mysterious
and terrible
disease.*

—William Arnot, Leaves of Gold

Focus on Faith

I need to be aware of the symptoms of envy. When I fail to share a friend's happiness over his good fortune, envy may be creeping into my being. When a disparaging remark slips from my lips as a colleague receives a compliment, envy may be tempting me. Instant treatment is required! One remedy is praising God for the good fortune of others and for the goodness that is in my own life.

Kris felt like she had been punched in the solar plexus when her sharing of good news in a group of friends was met with a hostile retort from Sara: "Why would she invite *you*?" Envy delivered the blow swiftly and unkindly. Kris was devastated, and it showed.

Later, she wished she had just smiled and walked away from the conversation. Others in the group would have understood that the comment spewed from Sara's habitual envy of others' gifts. Brushing off another's envy robs it of its potentially destructive power.

Never allow anyone
to rain on your parade
and cast a pall of gloom
and defeat on the entire day.
Nothing external
can have any power over you
unless you permit it.

—Og Mandino

Count to 10; take deep breaths; walk away. There are many means to counter the unpleasantness of envy when it is voiced in hurtful ways. Which one will I choose the next time envy raises its ugly voice?

Tom and Jake had competed with each other since childhood—in sports, the classroom, jobs, even for girlfriends. Vying with one another continued while working for the same company. Jake didn't like the way he envied Tom—after all, they were friends.

After years of dealing with occasional envy, Jake tried something different. He began differentiating between envy and regret. He regretted that he often fell behind Tom but refused to allow his regret to slide into envy. He also acknowledged that Tom's abilities often challenged him to reach higher skill levels.

Rejoice

in your
brother's progress
and you will
immediately
give glory
to God.

—St. John Chrysostom

To appreciate and admire the good fortune of others is to acknowledge God's gifts to them. If I desire to have such gifts to become a better person and to contribute to a better world, that is good. However, when my desire slips from appreciation to resentment at another's good fortune, danger lurks in the form of envy. Envy leads me away from God and toward self.

Acknowledging the grip of envy is a step toward wholeness. Now, we can begin resisting this trait that keeps us focused on self rather than God. Forgiving oneself for being envious opens the door to allow God's healing mercy to enter into our hearts.

Furthermore, gratitude for the many gifts God has given us—rather than focusing on those of others—keeps that door open.

With gratitude
in your hearts,
sing psalms,
hymns, and
spiritual songs
to God.

—Colossians 3:16

Focus on Faith

Lord, keep me mindful of the many gifts
you have given me—abilities, health,
wisdom, strengths. When I feel a twinge
of envy, I will stop to thank you for the
goodness in my life. Amen.

Forgiveness is essential for Christian growth. Refusing to forgive impedes God's presence in our lives and diminishes our ability to love. Jonathan wasn't the husband Emily expected. She envied her friends' marriages. Envy, in turn, made her hostile and angry.

Emily finally realized that she must forgive Jonathan, and accept him for who he is. Little by little, with daily prayer, she began to forgive. She also began to forgive herself for having judged her husband. Forgiveness led to addressing the problems that flawed their marriage.

If we wish to
be judged mercifully,
we must ourselves
be merciful toward
those who have
offended us.
We shall **be forgiven**
to the degree
that we **have forgiven**.

—St. John Cassian

Help me to look within myself,
Lord, to discover the roots of envy.
Show me where I can use your gift
of forgiveness to cultivate love and
joy where envy and bitterness lurk.
Amen.

Nothing changes life for the better as much as praising God and giving thanks—thanks and praise for *whatever* faces us right now, whether it is good or not so good! We must be thankful even for what we may secretly envy in another person. It's difficult to praise God and be filled with thanks and also be envious. Just try!

Praise God, from whom
all blessings flow;
Praise Him,
all creatures here below;
Praise Him above,
ye heavenly host;
Praise Father, Son,
and Holy Ghost.

—*Thomas Ken*

Praise God for the person who evokes envy in you. Thank God for the gift you observe in him or her. If it seems appropriate, pray for that gift for yourself.

You are not alone in being challenged by envy. The saints also experienced a touch of its venom on the path to holiness. The same path beckons us all, and along the way, God equips us with the tools we need to transform the ugliness of envy into the beauty of generosity. In this way, we participate in God's creation of all that is good.

Are you envious because I am generous?

—Matthew 20:15

Focus on Faith

It is said that feelings are neither right nor wrong—they simply are. That is true up to a point. However, feelings of envy that are left untended can grow like weeds, choking out healthy relationships and creating havoc. Lord, help me to be honest with what I am feeling, so that your grace can recondition my soul with your generosity.

We apply sunscreen before spending the day outside. We buckle our seat belts before venturing onto the expressway. Preparing to encounter envy is equally important for our spiritual and emotional health.

Be aware of the situations and the individuals that spark envy within you. When you know an encounter is coming, prepare with prayer. Thank God for your awareness. Praise God for the gifts "temporarily on loan" to *all* God's children.

What do you have that you did not receive? And if you received it, why do you boast as if it were not a gift?

—1 Corinthians 4:7

Imagine yourself in an envy-inviting situation—a party in an over-the-top lavish home or a day with a care-free friend who is joyful even though his life is quite difficult. Talk to yourself about how you might prepare for such an encounter without yielding to envy.

Ever think you'd like to change the world? Consider how the world might look if envy were erased from the planet. Nations wouldn't start wars because of envy over other countries' oil reserves or boundaries. Teens wouldn't shoot each other because of envy over a pair of shoes. Bullies wouldn't torment because they wouldn't envy the status of others.

Abolish envy within each heart, and change the world!

If envy
were a fever,
all the world
would be ill.

—Danish proverb

Focus on Faith

Lord, I know I cannot change the world by myself. However, with your help, I might change one little corner of my world—one street address, one work location, one person at a time. I will look for the good in another. I will not envy what they have or who they are, but will praise you for who they are, and for who I am—for we are all one in you. Amen.

About the Author

Patti Normile *is a former hospital chaplain, teacher, author, retreat director, and the writer of numerous* CareNotes *and* PrayerNotes. *She is the author of several books, including* Prayers for Caregivers.

Focus on Faith Series